These Days of Simple Mooring

New and Selected Poems

Florence Weinberger

BLUE LIGHT PRESS ◆ 1ST WORLD PUBLISHING

SAN FRANCISCO ◆ FAIRFIELD ◆ DELHI

Winner of the 2022 Blue Light Book Award
These Days of Simple Mooring
Copyright ©2022, Florence Weinberger

All rights reserved. Printed in the United States of America. No part of this book may be used or reproduced in any manner whatsoever without written permission except in the case of brief quotations embodied in critical articles and reviews. For information contact:

BLUE LIGHT PRESS
www.bluelightpress.com
bluelightpress@aol.com

1st WORLD PUBLISHING
PO Box 2211
Fairfield, IA 52556
www.1stworldpublishing.com

BOOK & COVER DESIGN
Melanie Gendron
melaniegendron999@gmail.com

COVER AND INTERIOR ART
"Anna Akhmatova" by Amedeo Modigliani, 1911
(Public Domain)

AUTHOR PHOTO
Alexis Rhone Fancher

FIRST EDITION

Library of Congress Cataloging-in-Publication Data

ISBN: 978-1-4218-3523-5

Acknowledgments

With deep appreciation, I wish to thank the following journals and anthologies in which some of these poems appeared, some in altered form, language, and/or titles:

Antietam Review, Apercus, Askew, Baltimore Review, Blue Unicorn, Comstock Review, Corridors, Cultural Weekly, Deronda Review, Epoch, Ghosts of the Holocaust, Hummingbird, I-70, Literature Today, Main Street Rag, Mantis, Midwest Quarterly, Miramar, Nimrod, North American Review, Pacific Coast Anthology, Pandemic Puzzle Poems, The Pedestal, Phantom Seed, Plainsongs, Poetry Kanto, Poetry Nook, Rattle, Rockvale Review, Salt, Serving House Journal, Shenandoah, Solo Nuevo, Spillway, and *Square Lake.*

Contents

What We Did Sundays During the War	1
What the Survivors Said to Us	2
American Buffalo	3
My Very Own Opera	4
Anniversary Tango	5
Bird Watch	6
Bishop's Lull	7
Whole Grains and Hard, Harmonious Ways	8
Mother's Blood	9
My Very Own Opera – Act Two	10
My Daughters Tell Their Friends	11
Mild Disturbances After Reading Kim Addonizio	12
Reflections Off a Dome in Florence	13
Jessie Drives Me Around in Tuscany	14
Trending	16
Rapport	17
To a Hawk That's Landed on My Deck	18
Some Things I've Not Done	19
Where I Was When Yitzhak Rabin Was Assassinated	20
To Write a Poem of Witness	21
A Common Grayness Silvers Everything	22
Trying to Flutter Leaves in China	24
Why Do You Travel	25
Roped	26
Iguazu Falls	27
A Modicum of Heartburn	29
Nascent January, 2018, After Rain	30
The Ritualists	31
If It's Only Breath	32
A Woman With a Lost Name	33
Stand Still	34
If I Understand the Theory of Punctuated Equilibrium…	35
The Prescription	36

Winter Comfort 37
The Medium is the Messenger 38
Renew Us to the Mercy of Lyres and Flutes 39
The End of Timing 40
Inspiration 41
Unraveling Darkness 42

The Invisible Telling Its Shape

I'm Not Playing Around 45
Summer School 46
She Began at the Ground 48
Perilous 49
The Heiress 50
Breaking Habits 51
Artifice 52
Ejaculate Trajectory I, II, III 53
Maybe This is About Smoke 54
The Stump 55

Breathing Like A Jew

From Where the Feet Grow 59
Mame Loshen, The Mother Tongue 60
The Power in My Mother's Arms 61
Mouth 63
Survivor 65
He Wears Old Socks 66
Suspects 67
The Light Gatherers 68
Angles 70

Sacred Graffiti

Agapanthus, Jacaranda, Bougainvillea 73
Thinking About 75
Step Into the Mojave at Noon 76

Humming	77
Revisiting Ozymandias	78
Landscape With Wounded Bird	79
Hitchhiker	80
From a Penitent's Hand	81
Wings	82
You Remind Me of Someone	83
Marrowbones	85
Anguish	86
The reason I don't visit your grave	87
Deep Inside the Silence I Hate, the Silence I Love	89
Smoking With My Father	90
Honeydew in Season	91
Boxing the Beast	92

Ghost Tattoo

My Mother's House	95
We've Taken Care of Everything	96
Caesarean Birth, Mid-Twentieth Century	97
My two daughters drop me off at the museum	98
Zachary's Rainbow	99
Mystics and Mathematicians Crowd the Shore	100
Stephen Hawking's Reasoning	101
The Critical Angle of Sunlight	102
Picasso's Four Bulls	103
Masks	104
Shoe Confessions	105
Lunatics Love Neruda	106
Nameless Flowers, Anonymous Trees	107
Announcement	108

About the Author	111

These Days of Simple Mooring

What We Did Sundays During the War

In the early forties, few people owned a car, and if you had one,
you hardly used it, because gas was rationed.
If you had one and could afford to, you went for a ride on Sundays.
Otherwise, you went for a walk.

Every Sunday, we went for a walk, my mother and father,
my sister and I. Over the bridge, past Starlight Park, up the hill,
around the corner to visit cousin Benny, my father's nephew,
on Benny's father's side.

Benny was a doctor, but we got to call him Benny. There was a
stoop, a waiting room for patients, Benny's office, a kitchen.
We never got past the kitchen, but there must have been
bedrooms, a bathroom.

I hung out in the waiting room; it was piled with magazines
I never saw anywhere else, like Esquire. When it was a sick visit,
I was brought into the office and sat up on the exam table.
On Sundays, we came into the kitchen, drank coffee, ate strudel.

Benny's mother, aunt and uncle lived there, somewhere in the
mystery of the rear. Benny's aunt made the strudel.
I was told they were refugees. His Uncle Martin
had a wife and children he hoped to bring out after the war.

Martin, Benny's uncle on his mother's side, was a photographer.
He loved taking pictures of our family. He even took one of
my sister sitting on the exam table in Benny's office. We'd
glue those pictures into our family album.

After the war ended, we'd still walk to Benny's on Sundays.
His mother and his aunt and uncle sat in the kitchen, silent and
somber. His aunt no longer offered us coffee and strudel.
Uncle Martin stopped taking our pictures.

What the Survivors Said to Us

We went to greet them and we clutched them to us,
the sluggish tide of cousins who staggered off the planes at Idlewild
or the boats in Hoboken like shell-shocked veterans,
speaking only Yiddish, and I,
with enough Yiddish left from childhood, listened to their stories,
how some survived by luck and some by guile and a few by kindness,
and I listened to their lingering nightmares.
After a while, when they no longer needed to relive them, when
they could ease their thoughts into their newly-learned language,
they told me what they had heard of the American dream.

American Buffalo

He never told me who gave him the Buffalo nickel
he clung to as the ship that brought him to America
eased into its berth. Maybe it was hiding
in a box of used clothes his uncle sent his parents.
Maybe the thugs who looted their apartment
after they were rounded up and sent to the ghetto
found it, and thought it worthless, and threw it away.
Maybe it was all the luck he had left after he was freed
from the death camp and made his way home.
It was all he kept. During long days crossing an ocean,
he shoved his European garments out of a porthole window,
one by one, arriving with the clothes on his back,
holding on to the nickel like a seed.

My Very Own Opera

Like a bird of prey, I graze the crowded air, its cacophony, its
absentmindedness. Like a predatory goshawk, I snatch its songs,
every note I ever heard becomes the beat I walk to, stalking hymns,
trumpet riffs, uncomplicated cadences of nursery rhymes, the hits,
the scales, the Tennyson poem I memorized in fourth grade. Music
gives me strokes I grow, like stitches on knitted scarves; I need
texture, gauge, the timeless measures that live under my breath.
A cantor's wail becomes a lullaby my father sang which kicks off
Queens' *Bohemian Rhapsody* which triggers *La Boheme*, shaky
bridges over troubled waters. It's all in the shuffle.

Librettos flicker through memory like Hollywood sound tracks.
Some die on my tongue, some pop like a late autumn crocus.
A dance I sat out while the thin girls tangoed,
the silly school anthem I sang, tears in my eyes.
These haunt the present:
a fierce Hallelujah, a graveside lament.
A phrase fell out of an open window, Gregorian chanting in a
church in Jerusalem made me mute. My feet tap them out, each
composed of something ravishing or so out of reach
the sound I'm making is akin to grieving.
Anyone passing by could hardly know
which song he danced me to on our wedding day.

Anniversary Tango

On your death anniversary, a ritual candle
        thick wax, wick cocked like an antenna

its flame flickering on my kitchen walls
        sears a wistful dance into this year's ledger

wedding bells long stilled
        broken wedding vows

woven into this morning's observance
        I think of you and another in the same hour

Death the betrayer gives me the right to betray
        because even myths harbor their shadows

I fold darkness into the light, a song I heard sung
        in an ancient tongue

all of us dancing together heartbeat to heartbeat
        the dead, the betrayed

the ones who confess, the ones who abstain,
        the ones who find love in the muck-up

Bird Watch

Ever since my conceit that you died into a bird – or rather many birds – I spotted you in every sparrow, gull, and starling. I felt protected, reminded. You'd go away from time to time, maybe to visit a child, a wife from a past life. This morning the skies were hushed and vacant, you were nowhere.......wait. O God, was that you, the red-tailed hawk squatting on my deck, pecking at a butchered rabbit? Once or twice the hawk raised its head, yellow eyes staring straight at me, broad wings at rest. Could those dark rufous feathers, that mottled chest, be harboring a shard of your being? I always thought you were more song than claw. I catch the stain of blood on its beak, tip of wing beginning to rustle. I see it soaring. Foraging. That *was* you: fierce, determined to survive, some days a little piece of my heart in your mouth.

Bishop's Lull

All things loved are pursued and never caught:
a line I sponged from Dean Young for its frisson of rue.

Made me think of cats at first,
then grown children who slip away, or the biggest fish

or sorrow, a kind of generic grief spill
sifted and culled until it pinned the lover I caught and kept so long

because I could not decide if my love was immortal
or would wither over the coming summer.

So it wasn't missing kids that gave me pause.
It was Bishop's lull, before she unhooked the fish

the fish imperiled by the heat in her hands
remorse coursing through her

but sometimes the catch needs a longer pause, maybe
decades, to unravel how much was love, how much was flak.

What I would have lost, had I let him go.

Whole Grains and Hard, Harmonious Ways

My mother knew heat, she'd hold her palm above the pot
to gauge the force and virtue of the flame. In her wrist,
the heft of black pepper, the troth of flour and eggs.
She knew marrow and garlic, hard harmonious ways
of healing, some days with sugar, some with bitter herbs.
And lying, that, too, buying a blouse, washing it
before wearing it so my father would think it was used
but he was rarely fooled,
he knew when her stew lacked character; he knew her.

Now that I no longer cook the way she taught me,
leaving out fat, adding whole grains, foods
she never understood, like kabocha squash and artichokes,
I still have left what is probably in my DNA; the smallest taste
is enough to implicate my nerves and all my senses.
She also taught me how to serve.
Pleasing a man is not always what it's for. While I add to the mix
I take the measure of time.
What's mine was my mother's first. How do I spend these final years?

Mother's Blood

My mother's myths are real and drenched with blood.
Cotton came in rolls then; rough-edged

pieces torn off, tucked inside her underwear,
and secretly discarded.

Surely she bled in steerage.
Bled her first child down the toilet.

A transcendent cook, she deftly handled sharp knives,
real steel that hacked through hard times, slit

finger tips.
From the small side of an ancient box grater,

blood flew off her knuckles as she reduced to shreds
phallic chunks of horseradish

for Passover, droplets mixed with beets
she'd add for color, and we all tasted the sting.

Patched my scraped knees. Drained meat to kosher it.
Flecks of blood pocked her face every time my father

diminished her, rouged her cheeks the day she told me
I'd become a woman.

My Very Own Opera – Act Two

Every day there's a hum in the day sometimes a fly bickering with the smell of my sun block two black holes colliding tires wobbling bikers revving egos couldn't miss the suss of fog the click of dog nails on pavement that's when the afflicted earth breaks into its solo I try to belt it out and out comes a mix of every song I ever heard going back to Swanee's longing hearts and heartless overseers a banjo'd buzz a mood switch to Protestant hymns I'm taught in school most of the kids Jewish and all the teachers Irish Missus Rolla setting lyrics to Saint Saëns isn't what caused static that's a broken friendship sound a scrape unlike the way the hissy hush erasers made of cotton batting scraps would shush the ice cream truck's bells suck us out the window hell I sang a cappella no one told me I couldn't rock a tune so now when drifters sneak up behind me catch me singing arias made of teeth and ruminations so disgraceful they could be a blue chorus line I tarry briefly they've already passed thinking I'm old I'm tuneless walk the tarmac not the beach the whale songs too real for revelation until the wail I hear leaps sea miles of mind play annihilates my happy birthday my very own bullet-proof opera something in my song sings a note I can hardly bear.

My Daughters Tell Their Friends

Hazard hums under my skin while I'm waiting in line
to pay for the figs,
get them home before they wither and lose their immaculate scent.

The windshield wiper swats the grime. Saves the wavering
bike rider when the sun begins its blinding afternoon descent.
I get home in a light sweat.

Through the porous walls, I overhear my daughters tell their friends
Mother's as strong as she was at forty,
she won't need bedpans or interpretation,

she won't need us taking her in,
dragging us away from our own lives,
she'll stay lucid and vibrant and self-reliant until the day she dies.

There's no way I'm going to admit orchids bring tears to my eyes,
the sun makes me sneeze,
some markets destabilize my pulse.

Mild Disturbance After Reading Kim Addonizio

At 5PM one afternoon I said to myself
it's time to bake my potato

and couldn't think why it sounded dirty.
I had been reading Kim Addonizio

and wanted to talk to her about orgasms
how it doesn't matter

once you're past eighty
unless you have a young lover

which I don't, and don't want
anymore.

I had a friend
whose lover was younger than her kids.

He would eat their bananas
and forget to replace them.

It's the same with the old ones,
who forget.

Living alone, baking potatoes,
setting the table for one,

I bless this harsh freedom, no one
to pass me the sour cream.

Pass me the sour cream, I say to myself.

Reflections Off a Dome in Florence

Maybe it's the longing that contains the power,
not its fulfillment, the Sphinx by now too effaced,
the pyramids too ubiquitous for imagination.

My neighbors have moved to Barcelona, so
they'll have the Picassos. I miss elephants,
dust and elegance, the tiger slink into the long grasses.

My daughter stands at a window in Florence,
snaps and clicks *send*; hunger singes me the way
sun sizzles off the campaniles, the Arno's waters.

The years I wandered, skimmer with a camera,
I lived hours where lives were counted in centuries.
I said I went. Now I stay home, reflections

working off the glint, off souvenirs in my
reverie: a poke among the gravestones in Donegal,
a conversation with an old tailor

on the Isle of Capri, of all places.

My Daughter Drives Me Around in Tuscany

Looking back, castles and Chianti
common as gelato, our silence
or comments in terse monosyllables

at first screened the tension, then
slowly dissolved it as you drove with
ease up toward the high walled towns

back roads unraveled where olive trees
wavered and galaxies of sunflowers
grinning their clown colors

made us stop and pose
next to their heliotropic faces
then what may have looked aimless

driving past tangled grapevines
we talked away some of that past
let some simply pass

so we couldn't miss
the accidental restaurant
talk like long time friends about

a simple sauce of fresh tomatoes
olive oil, basil, something more
the village fair we chanced on

the generous cheese man slicing samples
until I sense what you want to remember
what you want to show me

as if in a previous life
you'd already planned this life
in order to find your way back

hoped to show me
how you're at home here
where I've never been before

yes, I see now
there is more than one home on earth
more than one journey to get there

Trending

The reproductive behavior of hermaphroditic fishes is diversified
	and unpredictable, but neither they nor
parthenogenetic lizards are known to practice shaming.

Asexual bacteria are everywhere. Regarding virgin births,
	some scorpions and water fleas do not need sperm to reproduce.
Only political cultures insist sexes are distinguishable by their genitalia.

Human reproduction, a lower form of evolution, is tame by comparison.
	My grandchildren have matured, along with our complex
technologies, but human reproduction has not changed much.

	Who will teach them the dance of the feathers and the drum?

Rapport

When I ask the boy whether he needs warm socks,
he asks for *The Call of the Wild*
so the next time I see him
caged and crazed in the hospital's wing
where the teens are kept,
I bring him a copy of Jack London's novel.
Every visit after that I want to fit the words he babbles
to some narrative I can follow, but we do not reach rapport
until he confides *I am Buck. This is my story.*
My heart runs toward him.
We both hear the howling in the next room.

To a Hawk That's Landed on My Deck

indifferent
your stare your

stand
on the body of death

rat rabbit or
clumped darkness

nothing to rescue, as if
I'd match my courage to your claws

I've known your hover
settled, you have no song

stirred breast feathers, stilled wings
grounded here as I am

eating a dull meal
left to clear the remains

of what you brought down
in the pecking order of prey and necessity

what will I tear with my bare hands
when there is everything to rage about

Some Things I've Not Done

I've not killed the perpetrator
I've not stood outside his house
        brick wrapped in parchment
I've not sent cash to the outposts
I've not told my daughters
I've not sold everything
I've not knelt
I've not risen above it
I've not planted
        or flaunted
I've not engaged my neighbor
I've not said here, you can sleep in my bed
I've not traced the names on the wall
I've not brought matches

What I have done

I have made more lists
I have begun to weep

Where I Was When Yitzhak Rabin Was Assassinated

Isn't it beautiful, my friend said, of forged Rome, ersatz
Egypt. Near Venice, a volcano erupted without consequence.
Isn't it beautiful, he gushed, as we passed a bloodless
Broadway in the Las Vegas sleight-of-hand.

Brooklyn's expat waitress tells us her mother's been waiting
eons for a grandchild, and in Bally's casino, a sailor on leave
waits with one heart and four spades. In my agnostic soul,
none of it is beautiful, so

while my friend spun and nickeled for gold, I sheltered in my
hotel room, the air falsely chilled, desert sun glinting off
the television screen. I was betting on a royal flush, gambling
the remote would turn up a foreign film with readable subtitles.

Natural Born Killers, Batman Returns, Terminator 2. Not a
Bergman or Fellini in sight. Car ads, dancing raisins, six
couples sucking each other's genitalia; not my jackpot.
Yitzhak Rabin has been assassinated.

Unreal. That clichéd word unreeled, replayed until I was certain
this was not an attack by Martians under a false sky in a fake city.
It was the holy city of Jerusalem, where God holds the chips.
Where was I when the one wild throw went so wrong,

when a man of peace bet and lost. A single toss:
the history of the world shifts, and the Middle East roils for
decades. I am in the city of chance, city of sham and amnesia.
I never asked my friend what he came here to forget.

To Write a Poem of Witness

you need a heart cold as an ice floe bearing an elder out to sea
not the fever of a people scorched then scattered
their grammar left at border crossings
where the language shifts so the word for water
doesn't quench and bread and dead are cynical rhymes
and the earth's holy hum ends with a coda bleeding like a raped mouth.
Sometimes my voice is so hoarse from crafting metaphors
it stutters, like an excuse.

A Common Grayness Silvers Everything

On days like this, the Pacific passive as a pond,
a goose-down cloud-cover over the dun hills,
we may not miss the sun at all,
      its rictal grin and the way it gilds
slicks of spit and grease on the tarmac.

Diane Arbus and Ansel Adams, knowing sun
could burn a shot or singe a cornea,
      worked with black and shades of gray,
savoring grades of distinction.

Once the sun's graze was out of their eyes,
they could illuminate freaks, lodgepole pines,
      leach out any hint of pigment,
even when summers blazed into conflagrations
or bleakness eclipsed objectivity.

What you saw is earth's flea market, medlies
      of treasures lit up by light left over
when the sun subsides, click after click,
      shadow reinvented as
matte bark, rock silhouette, silvered earthworm.

Don't you remember *The Grapes of Wrath*,
mud on their tires when they finally reached
      the promised land, windows
smudged with a continent of grime, dirty faces,
white teeth, some semblance of a hopeful grin.

Gray was the way Dorothea Lange uncovered
the muck of southern poverty, Helen Levitt
      the faces of children who didn't laugh.

How Roman Vishniak's spackled grays
foretokened smoke drifts over the crematoria,

though I heard the hopeless kept a memory of the
glow, slow heat that wouldn't burn, but warmed,
      a sun that sanctified the ruins,
filled the crevices on dark nights, and loved back
the morning light.

Trying to Flutter Leaves in China

Deemed too antique to be abroad where breezes spread presumptive
death, I have been indoors by decree. I'd rather die in my time,
my body worn to the end of its destiny.

Friends bring me sustenance. I swallow godliness. Yet the walls
shudder me awake to the ruined familiar. I must open the doors to try.
Put on my shoes.

I step out disguised, yet recognized. They know my gait, my hat,
the bland mask I wear, so they nod or wave. The ones that go uncovered
look unconcerned. A few smirk.

I stare at them, a third grade teacher practiced in shaming
but when I see they are impervious or humorless, I revert to my
soul animal, I growl and spew, I stop wearing white.

My guise now is black and conspicuous, I glare to disturb,
toll the bells of black death, heart of darkness, robes of judgment, crows
divining from the tops of telephone poles.

When I see my stunt has not stung them to contrition, I become
unsubtle, hiss the word so it skitters in their direction, but still they insist
on sanctifying their ignorance.

The earth moves of its own volition. I was told my breath could flutter
leaves in China. I am merely seeking to ruffle my neighbors, not
the ones who bring me apples. The ones who cry in their sleep.

Why Do You Travel?

asks the New York Times, and 676 people email them photographs which zing to my email, each a landscape or legend sent from the world of people with open eyes who open their lenses and snap what they love when it signals with tingles, from single rocky outcrops and desert vistas to cowboys and shoppers, revelers and trains, trash piles and pilgrims, blazing decorations, gray schist, rivers and icons, parades and carnivals, wild faces and lined faces, the silos, the frenzied horses, cooks and caravans where gypsies tented and repaired broken pots, my longing stirred for what I will never jump off, climb into or onto, or risk in countries run by informants, dictators, fanatics, but thank you, NYT, for showing me people grinning, walking and riding, praying and swimming, posing and clicking, eating and kissing, hefting potatoes, planting rice, sifting beans, selling umbrellas and flowers, trinkets, you showed me sleepy cobras, sheep with funny faces, baby elephants nursing, rainbows vying with hot air balloons, the convergence of two rivers, rituals and iguanas, drums, green champagne bottles, frescoes in Umbria. Thank you for taking me to Umbria, to a mosque in Casablanca. Thank you for leaving out cracking glaciers, hacked limbs, wandering populations, the disgraced, the hanging burning despairing lifers, druggies, serial killers. Bullet holes on government buildings. Thank you for thrilling me with spewing volcanoes, saintly monks and cities on stilts, lions and replicas of Viking ships, women carrying encyclopedias of freight on their heads, romantic bridges, bakery windows, reef cuts and sand dunes, zebras and sleeping dogs, the Kurama fire festival, the Kazakh eagle hunters, spiders and bicycles and at last, Positano. Thank you for reviving the places I've been: Ha Long Bay, Varanasi, Agra, Paris, Venice, London, Rajasthan, Florence, Seville, Giza, Chicago, Madrid, Las Vegas, Cancun, Mont Saint Michel, Angkor Wat, Galway, Vancouver, Jerusalem, Needles, Bar Harbor, Sedona, Hong Kong, Rome, Kyoto, Kuala Lumpur, Provincetown, Phnom Penh, Brooklyn. I know why you go; I went to taste the noodles, to sense the other, to break my cycles, to savor my delirium, to buy something useless and something local.

Roped

I went to return with evidence.
I hung a camera around my neck, outing myself, an innocent
trying to catch flutters at their edges.
To find something worthy of the journey, to a country rife with ruins.
Worth the film, the flash, the light itself,

if I could peel the bland skins off the still goods,
reveal the hands that made those cargo nets,
carved the wood canes that seemed ready to sprout if planted,
twisted the ropes hanging from a beam, breadths and lengths
like penises in the clubby showering after a ball game

but without the vigor and the curses,
an old man with a dingy beard and wet eyes standing next to them.
Caught by the careless artifice of his handiwork,
I began snapping, seeking enough accretion to generate symmetry,
the strands that hold the gift-wrapped universe together,

my mother tying ropes around the cartons
before the hired hands came and moved us to another apartment
where we got a month's free rent, my patiently seething mother
tugging hard to make sure the knots held
and after the movers left, unpacking and hanging everything up,

even the pictures,
breaking down the cartons
and dragging them to the trash bins
and saving the rope and having dinner on the table that night
when my father got home from work.

Iguazu Falls

    As if all the gods have slashed their wrists at once,
                      your inexhaustible waters pour and pour,
    diminishing brooks, drowning rivers, flooding creeks,
                              maddening lakes.

    You dry the deserts, drain the plains,
        slurp up puddles and ponds,
                inhale clouds before they drop their moisture,
a tsunami swallowing its mother.

You are greed snagging runoff, grabbing mountains,
                sweeping streams from the foothills, stealing sorrow
from the ice melt.

You are mercy, giving shelter to Taroba,
        who stole Naipi from the vengeful snake god Mboi;
           sealed them in after-death tree-pierced stone
    deep inside the Devil's Throat.

Even as I praise you, you embarrass my voice.
        Even as I face you from the safety of concrete and iron,
      I feel hurricanes in your trumpet, tornadoes in your blow,
beauty's menace spewing like bullets.

    You split rocks
    and countries, handicap language,
                batter feet that seek traction,
    sing excessively.

    Your lust does not diminish.

You command us, and we come, on buses and planes, we gawk,
we rent boats, get soaked; we sputter, we giggle with fear;

                      we cannot see you clearly,
          cannot take you in, cannot take a single photograph that
                    contains you.
We skirt you, fly over you, put you on the internet,
                    we are so silly, so small. So in love.

A Modicum of Heartburn

About a year ago
I started to fall in love.

Fortunately there's a plank on the second landing with a handrail
made out of balsa wood, which I've heard is stronger
than pine, hickory or oak, and as I stopped to take a breath

there stood a candy man handing out free samples.

He offered gin or Snickers.

Once I dreamt of having parallel lives;

I could bake a pie while lying on my back,
but the road not taken was already taken.

Like Hemingway, who left a sentence undone
so he could kick-start his fictions in the morning,
I go to bed prepared to skip straight to the victory lap,

but when I get up, and the sun also rises,
I'm still on the second landing, the stairs waxed to splinters,
the bannister slick with sap, and the candy man's out of Snickers.

Nascent January, 2018, After Rain

What a disappointment this century has been – so far.
                                             David Bowie

This morning, after rain, I saw half a rainbow.
I mean, it aspired, it rose and spread and headed
higher, but instead banged into a cloud bank where
it got stopped dead.
              The roll out, though, was impressive,
bloody reds and purples and yellows; it was enough
rainbow for me. Perfected rainbow would have asked me:
                    of what you are given, what do you give?

The Ritualists

Be patient that I address you in a poem; there is no other fit medium.
                                      W. C. Williams

It was in Baja I first saw horses running on the beach.
Though they had riders, I was moved by the freedom they implied,
and the incongruity. The next time I saw them – how apt they are,
on second thought, in landscapes of water – a few

cantering, others being led, I was in California and you said
they were out for exercise, as we were, and I marveled that this was
a daily occurrence where you could pause on your walk and watch
any time you wanted.

Because of the rain, the camellias were budding early that year,
even before my birthday, which we always celebrated by eating well
and drinking martinis, yours vodka, mine gin, two olives apiece,
toasting our taste for gossip and witch lore and general wickedness.

I guess that's why you went on smoking after the rest of us quit,
insisting smokers were much more interesting.
I didn't take that personally. Apparently you felt
I had distinction enough to amuse.

Everyone knew you differently. Old gems smoked at your neck,
jade on your earlobes, opals when you spoke. Without flash,
you retold their Georgian histories, their Victorian sublimations,
the careless promiscuity of families

that let them go. With gesture and myth, you guarded your privacy.
We met infrequently, but always on our birthdays. When I smoked,
I was moderate, five, six cigarettes a day.
When I quit, the day kept those five or six black holes.

If It's Only Breath

Think about the air you set in motion.

If it's only breath.

If it's more, if it's a word, if it breaches an ear,
if the core of your breath bores
into the world body:
think about that.

Think about bringing the knowledge of waiting.
Before the sprung thought, the skill of the pause.

You may begin to understand composure.
You will enjoy the mastery.

A Woman With a Lost Name

A woman with a lost name took brown into her mouth:
roan, dun and chestnut, burnt umber.

Tasted horse;
traced mane, hooves, withers, onto the dank rock canvas of her cave.

Her flanks quivered.
She drew in her cheeks, slicked her lips,
called on her body's wellspring. Spat. Scooped up drifts of sand,
eroded rock, dried blood of feral pig and bison.

Smeared into shape with a knot of her hair or the nibs of her fingers
the flaring things she saw down on the plain, and wanted to be.

Deep in these caves her horses kicked down the walls,
dug themselves out, and they ran, bearing on their sweat-hot backs
the women who otherwise tended the fires.

Who otherwise still would be there, waiting.

Stand Still

      Look over there. To your left
           just past the dune and that showy cluster
                  of rocks.

Don't you see where I'm pointing
                past the froth –
the fluke tips?
      The intermittent spray? Wait for them

to come up for air
      spilling the sea away
           from their skin, their young calves
    cavorting like kittens

and I promise you
the heed of those massive cows will haunt you
      like the ghost of your mother's vigilance
when she called you from play to the table.

Listen.
      When they whistle their babies home
the ancient and mythic songs you hear

           will shift forever your notion of worship.

If I Understand the Theory of Punctuated Equilibrium....

...there may have been a peaceful time. If there was plenty of corn,
no spears, flower dyes for face painting, everyone a child
without an alphabet.

According to the theory of punctuated equilibrium, stable periods
became raucous when something precipitous happened
to change the trajectory forever.

The wheat, the wheel, the ice freeze. A mutant gene,
a quake, a battle, things finally settle, sometimes
for decades,

before the next glitch, which looks like a minor shift
but when accreted to the present day, becomes huge.
Now it seems every day there's something new,

what robots do, what we do when we aggravate a forest's roots,
or steal from the earth
what doesn't belong to us.

The Prescription

He says
when your blood
turns sluggish
and sleepy
eat something salty.
Salt.
All these years
no salt.
I'd forgotten salt.
No Chinese food.
Canned chicken broth?
Are you kidding me?
I find one hidden
in the far corner
where canned goods expire
crack it open
heat it, eat it.
Slurp it like a kid.
It bites me like a loving old
toothless dog.
It licks me back home
to my mother's kitchen.
I don't compare
the slick of fat.
I don't care. I'm told
to eat salt, to taste
total recall, all the long history
of salt preservation
salt routes and
salt mines, salt wars
and salt water oceans
salt love coursing
through my blood
pumping, pumping.

Winter Comfort

sweetened with parsnips
roughs of knob celery
creviced by salt-parched failings

of unlived minutes
measured like confessions
whispered to a fissured wall

potato thickness of phone gossip
a squeeze of lemon for a gutless tweet
carrots instead of sticks

a Spanish onion
for thin-skinned days
rigor Neruda understood

paprika for passion, beans
for mirth, a bloody bone
for marrow

simmer like a thick novel
its complications boiled down
to a reckoning

a call to balance
with lovage or parsley or other
corrections

the long cooling
best reheated
in a chilly season

The Medium is the Messenger

My friend, who is a psychiatrist, scoffs
when I tell him I saw two clouds,
one dark, bristling with intimidation,
and next to it a fluffy white one, and
as I'm watching, the white cloud closes
over the dark one and gobbles it up.

Shouldn't it be *seven* white and *seven* dark,
he teases, referencing Pharaoh's dream,
the one that made Joseph prince of Egypt?
I get a scoff when I expect an inquisitive
eyebrow lift; he knows I'm not a prophet,
but hey, humor me for a minute.

Freudian that he is, fat cigars and pearly
clouds may just be facts, and nature
just nature banging up against nature –
pure coincidence – while I see the gods
flagging me: *look up, I am sending you
bouquets of white chrysanthemums.*

Renew Us to the Mercy of Lyres and Flutes

Where are this century's muses, have they abandoned their vocation,
are they hefting Berettas instead of bone flutes?

Can't we recall the damsels who flickered around Wedgwood pottery,
masterful Erato, creator of hilarious vocabularies made especially
       for lovers?

Polymnia, inventor of divine geometries and sacred grammars.
Let's get Thalia to tickle us to raucous laughter when Melpomene
       bemoans our desecrations.

Terpsichore – she'd remind us we once danced face to face.
Euterpe's lyrics could give us silence, so we hear, again,
cantatas above the clamor.

Urania holds a compass to the stars;
wouldn't that help us find our way back?
Shouldn't we beseech Clio, keeper of history,
not to canonize us killers of species and civil conversation?

And finally Calliope, the muse of justice, who inspired Homer to
turn history into epic poetry.

O let us become muse to the muses, prompters of peaceful alphabets.
Give them rooms of their own muted by cork-stilled walls,

dandelion wine, quill pens, reasons to write us with mercy,
                              once they have forgiven our deeds.

The End of Timing

What time we waste, wasting time.
                              Charles Wright

Watching the numbers fall and rise.
Cursing the fools. Counting the dying.

Seasons hardly change where I live. Wind has its way.
I walk where it tells me.

I sing a *niggun* made of syllables and hunger, a song
I sang to my infant child before she had words.

It is a song of ancient tradition I made up for this time.

I cannot reach my child by plane, I cannot reach her children.
Who of us will be reached in time?

Who will watch reruns, bring wine and butter lettuce to their
elderly neighbors?   Some will write wills.

Some will remember to practice their Czerny exercises,
unmask at last in front of an open window.

Inspiration

    Magnetism, she claims
    is the source
    of her inspiration.

Our earth's a gravid rock that begs
    to be punctured, probed and perceived.
    Confessed back to itself.

She gives it her mothered tongue

    dips its grudges, stropped cleavers,
    embers of dark inheritance
into a potion made of potent odes and madrigals.

    Ejecting its dead clichés
    its random brutalities

    she also dredges
    the poverty
    of alarmist speech.

Goes to the masters
and feasts on their warrior words.

    When she is sated
     she throws her engorged heart
     into the fire
and the shriven letters rise of themselves.

Unraveling Darkness

In the deep purples and supernal blacks of the Rothko Chapel
I sat back straight and tried to
shift from soul tourist to a self so accessible, each new breath

would subdue the impatience that awaited Rothko's promise,
or the invention I had made of it.

But his walls would not yield to me, not their contention and
not their consolation, would not slither off their verticals
to address my supplication.

Outside flared the light that shuns this coruscating darkness,
its gravity tugging.
I faltered when I left; thought it was the rebels in my knees.

Only years later, when solitude offered its gifts to me, did I see
how firmly orange rests on a pedestal of blue,

how a simple field of yellow binds red to gray and gray to jade,
and I was able to walk out into daylight torn open.

THE INVISIBLE TELLING ITS SHAPE

I'm Not Playing Around

A dozen scratches it takes
to stop him, a kick in the groin,
and I'm not above hair pulling
either, I'm this fierce
match scraping a sidewalk,
this kid, this eight-year-old kid
making herself visible.

Summer School

I play on a stoop
by myself   hot Bronx
summer   my mother
and sister indoors
friends at camp   in the
country   I never
knew how to refuse
a man who was lost
I tell him where a
neighbor lives   show me
he asks   we walk up
five flights   he's ahead
now   stops on the next
landing   drops his pants
hands me a penny
for ice cream   that scares
me   I know it costs
three cents   I say my
mother is calling
his voice soothing me
carries   a neighbor
hears us   comes out to
check   he pulls up his
pants and runs away
they call the police
I describe him   red
hair   freckles   I am
five   my mother takes
the penny   throws it
out the window   don't
we give you enough
I don't know it yet
but it's true   from that

day I will never
have enough   ice cream
or money or time
to tell how a sense
of danger grips me
when anything is
exchanged between me
and a stranger   coins
kind words   apples   then
possibilities
of love or friendship
pivot on what is
enough between us
how I uncover
intent   what I get
for my money   listen
my mother wasn't
calling me   I made
that up   I still lie
out of habit   or
to save my life   I
don't always know   can
you teach me trust   are
you sure that's a smart
idea   I'll taunt you
but the words will be
on my tongue   and if
you listen you'll hear
them   I'm a good girl

She Began at the Ground

She liked the symmetry of lattice,
recalled a road in Maui
flanked by eucalyptus trees,
a driveway paved with bricks
as consistent as fish bones.
She liked the geometric risks
taken by Frank Stella and Mondrian,
chevron, protractor and color
arrangements stamping her evenly
because she wanted balance,
like anyone who falls in love
too much, can't tell fish from
desire. She planted morning glory,
sweet peas and jasmine.
She planted all sorts of vines. They had
a tendency to wildness. She nailed them
to lattice, as they grew.

Perilous

Once I got in the habit of walking
with small stones in my hand, rubbing them
like bells, savoring them
with an uncontrollable smile, the invisible
telling its shape, I could hold that
instead of fear.
I want to say, I know shape
isn't what it seems, it's only container,
blood does live in stones.
Even as I write, my palm
at the percept of cold slick surface
comes alive, almost immersed in an icy stream.
My feet become used to slippery passage.
I want to say, this arises from tapping,
stone against stone,
but it really unfolds from story.
It was my mother lived near a moving stream,
stored wrapped meat in the flow to keep
fresh, crossed it barefoot and young.
Nothing was slippery then,
everything brimming,
America undreamed. The pebbles I find
in the gutter, at the curb, small worn shards
of river rock, decorate these
suburban lawns in orderly patterns.
Sprinklers wash them into the street.
I pass by, pick up two,
roll them like dice. Whatever comes up.

The Heiress

I keep one pot, and the lid
of a bushel basket she used
to kosher the meat for Passover.

They will change the configuration
of my house: already the pot
ages my kitchen, and the lid,

hung on the wall like found poetry,
reminds me of Chinese fishermen
who use what is at hand.

Breaking Habits

Maybe it's better to go to the back of a cave alone.
Scratch rage or leach the spectrum from vegetables,
paint animal worship on the walls.

All my life I've answered as if I had to.
Dense sentences swerving around the seed, nuanced
like slow-ripening peaches:
fiber, transparency, flavor, skin.
Some I ate,
gave some away,
and stayed hungry.

If love is guaranteed, can I learn to be still
so all of motion and stasis can meet in the throw of the coins
which I no longer have to carry?

So still, the chance pattern of milkweed filament landing
need never again be mysterious
and the Fool in the deck is free to fall off the cliff
in the wind's direction.

Maybe it's better to measure the length of this beach alone.
First in the morning to step off land's perimeter.
To study the sea lives stranded here.
To count only on the inevitable appearance
of dogs, husks, and wreaths of kelp.
To stop looking in your cards
for answers.

Artifice

How easy
to paint bamboo on walls

I cut acacia branches
bring them from the garden

In my crystal vase, apple blossoms
On the table, yellow dust

Ejaculate Trajectory I, II, III

A series of photographs by Andrès Serrano

He shoots streams of semen on a black field
so they spill and pool like sea foam
or gum like snot or rope like DNA. Interesting. Still, I doubt
he fully demonstrates the affect of contrast, the omen of audacity
or the consequence of desire
when he shows us these shimmering framed spews.

They could be a man's debate, like pissing in the snow,
or only Serrano's. One man's solution to the world's problems,
and damn, I find myself admiring the way he uses seed,
he doesn't stick it in the ground or plant it in
a woman for metaphor or carelessness, and
if he's only bragging, I don't mind, he made me wonder.

Hard to say what I would have done
with film and a wayward impulse, probably used my own cliché,
reached for blood, spread my legs and let it drip
thick enough to stain,
or sliced my finger with a kitchen knife, or spit
with equal fury, smeared the mess and prayed for humor.

Borrowed his title as if it's a spoonful of sugar,
as if I lived beside him
in some experimental marriage full of trial and sweetness.
Because I'd like to believe I'd end up agreeing with him,
which is the beauty of it, of randomness
shaken loose from what I thought I wanted.

Maybe This Is About Smoke

Maybe it's about a pipe I once bought you
                a briar encased
                in silver filigree, handmade and individual
                vacation photographs
                pipes in your right hand
                an elbow on a knee
                the dark cocoa smell
                of a special blend of tobacco
                Saturday afternoons, going out to buy tobacco
                from pushy Melinda
                who also sells chocolates
                and gives you free samples
Maybe it's about young waitresses and salesgirls, small
                noses twitching around you
Maybe it's about your hands
                filling a pipe, dipping it
                into a leather pouch
                tamping, lighting, drawing smoke, flavor
                the jolt, the fire
                my mother breathing through a respirator
                the doctor asking whether she ever smoked
                my father›s emphysema
                my inability to tolerate smoke
                my anger, your accommodation
                smoking after hours in the chilly garage
                before coming to bed
Maybe it's about polarity
Maybe it's about our relationship, how it clouds over
                how it becomes impacted
                turns to ashes, and reignites
Maybe it's about friction and residue and mastery
                what we breathe in each other›s
                presence, what dissolves
                what stays on the tongue, on the teeth
Maybe it's about my fear of losing you

The Stump

When we came back from the hospital,
when we came back and hardly spoke,
when we ate our evening meal
without hunger or imagination,
when we watched war news and went to bed
and slept, and woke with the need
and you pounded your way into me,
did you feel your shape?
Did it feel like the stump of your brother's leg
twitching with pain, seeking leverage?
Did you feel that phantom
reaching?
Did you feel me pushing to meet you?
Did you feel my panic?
Did you feel what that did to my desire?

BREATHING LIKE A JEW

From Where the Feet Grow

Curious how Yiddish won't translate easily
into American idiom so I can share with you
the graze of my father's judgment, but I knew
exactly what he meant when he said
She wants to know from where the feet grow.
I was someone who needed to find the hidden
wellspring of things; no answer would end it
once and for all, none would be perfect,
even come close; feet grow from inches,
from dresses, from socks and buttocks,
feet grow straight out of the flesh, they descend
from hems, they fall from ankles thick with sorrow,
slim with grace, they stick out naked in horses.
My father thought I wanted illumination.
I only wanted to hear him name me in Yiddish,
his voice modulated so I understood
how bemused he was by my brightness,
how charmed by my lust.

Mame Loshen, The Mother Tongue

Yiddish, my first language,
you were given to me whole, your wild colors
intact, your bent humor, centuries
of bottled-up rage and richly-imagined revenge.
How else could my father have heaped curses on
my mother with such violent originality, called
my dates names vicious enough to make me ashamed
I walked down the street with them.
And still I believed in him, believed
the wisdom he borrowed from ancient proverbs was his,
believed in his dazzling litany of dirty jokes,
believed in his gossip, believed in his criticism,
believed in the shop details of his paranoia,
believed in his poker-player's paranoia,
because out of this avalanche of language,
punctuated by deep painful rasps of breath
as he battled bronchitis and then emphysema,
still smoking those pungent Turkish cigarettes,
came the rhythm of my poems, like hard slaps
with an open palm, panic he would run out
of breath and die at the door of our third-
floor apartment, die in the middle
of a shout or a story, but
where in his mouth were the milk and the honey,
and where was his boyhood, and David's, and where was the
sheepherder's whistle calling down the steep slopes of Hebron
and where in his mouth were the biblical mothers
Sarah, Rebecca, Rachel and Leah and where
in his mouth was his own mother Rachel
who taught him the one song he sang to me
when I was a child?

The Power in My Mother's Arms

My mother stretched dough thin, thinner,
to its splitting edge.
All that certainty gripped her wrist,
while she sieved bread crumbs through her fingers,
    nuts, sugar, apples, lemon rind,
laying down family legends like seams in a rock; then
she rolled it all up the sweet length of the dining room table.

Beaten egg glazed the top, and still aroma to come,
                cooling and slicing.
I didn't mind her watching me eat;
I'd give back the heat of my need gladly, fuel to keep the cycle
elemental, if you've watched birds feed their young.

To every celebration, she matched a flavor, giving us memory,
giving exile the bite of bitter herbs.
God's word drifted in fragrant soups,
vigor in the wine she made herself, clear and original.

My mother's death changed the alchemy of food.
Holidays run together now like ungrooved rivers.
I forget what they are for.
I buy bakery goods.
They look dead under the blue lights.

I don't do anything the way she taught me.
I don't look like her and I don't sound like her,
    but I stand like her.

There must be rituals that sever
what harms our connection to the past
and lets us keep the rest.
If not, let me invent one from old scents and ceremonies.

Let me fashion prayer from a piece of dough, roll it out,
cut in the shape of my mother,
plump, soft, flour-dusted,
the way I once played cook with clay.
Let me keep the cold healing properties of female images,
their power to hold fire.
Let me bake her likeness in vessels made of earth and water.
Let me bless the flames that turn her skin gold,
her eyes dark as raisins.
Let me bless the long wait at the oven door.
Let me bless the first warm dangerous taste of love.
Let me eat.

Mouth

My mother is smitten with silence.
A woman kisses me on my mouth a moment before departure.
Stingy giver, who sends me this cropped dream,
like treasure jumbled with the dregs of dumpsters.

My mother grunts a few guttural sounds,
so I know she's had a stroke.
I pick her up and carry her, an uncommon charity in my arms.
I never knew whether she loved me;
she never said.

During the Great Depression of the Thirties,
when even words were spent judiciously, it became necessary
to understand the smallest gesture,
the tender way my daughter works with the deaf.
Holding her love

inside her body, she teaches her hands to speak,
while her eyes add nuance.
Her big soft brown eyes.
Those were the words I heard as the dream dissolved.

Now my grandchild empowers my mother's name, sees
through her eyes. But there's that shadow woman who kissed me
on the mouth and asked me to miss my boat.
Go home a different way, she said,
go home by way of Hong Kong.

She offered enchantment, a chance to shop, but I've been there,
I've eaten duck roasted in clay, breathed the hot air. Bought a
notebook, white pages, red lines. I keep my dreams in it. I'm
through shopping for other gods. When I sit cross-legged, fingers

touching, breathing in a deep Yoga breath, I exhale a Jewish sigh.
When I go to a medium, he conjures an Eastern European shtetl,
he produces an accent, he brings me my immigrant mother. It seems
she has changed, she's regained her speech, adopted American ways.

She says she approves of oyster white for my daughter's living room.
The fan in the bathroom, she says, needs to be oiled.
She says she has come this far to assure me she loves me,
and God is a woman.

Survivor

He knows the depths of smokestacks,
from their bleak rims down
their spattered walls, from their ash cones
to the bone-bottom ground.
Once he could see under skin,
inside the body, where deprivation
thins the blood of all desire
except hunger.
For years he wanted to forget
everything. He knows it is possible
to live only at the surface,
it is possible to work,
to marry and have daughters.
But his daughters
look like people he once knew,
and he dreams them.
He dreams them opening doors,
sending letters. When he wakes,
he knows he has been dreaming.
This year, he will show his daughters
where he was born. He will show them
the chimney, the iron gate,
the deep oven where his mother baked bread.

He Wears Old Socks

He wears old socks,
pajamas full of holes,
saves shoes, saves
everything, stuffs
large amounts of food
in his cheeks, chews
slowly. So much is
his. This is how
he once survived.
Now he has means
to buy new socks,
eat in restaurants.
It isn't that old habits
die hard, or memories.
It's the way he
represents the dead,
with his own bones,
not knowing
where the others lie.

Suspects

In the small Hungarian town of Szentendre,
        where artists and writers live,
my husband buys thirty-two pieces of strudel
        for his wife and his daughters.
He has come back after forty years.
He wants us to taste the substance of his return,
        he wants us gorged with freedom
and more sweets than anyone needs.
        We eat them all on the train to Belgrade;
butter glazes our lips and fingers.
        We become European, a family
eating on a train while the train
clatters through the countryside.
        At the Yugoslav border,
the train stops. The conductor slides open
        the compartment door, enters,
holds out his hand. He seems
        both old and young, careless, yet
well-trained. Stacking our passports
on top of one another, he shuffles them
        like a deck of cards, opens each one,
stares at our pictures. He matches the
        faces, his head bobbing up and down,
his eyes looking straight into ours.
        Hours seem to pass, perhaps even days
before he smiles, hands them back,
bows, and leaves. It takes us a long time
        to become a family again,
        to tell our jokes and hum the latest tunes.

The Light Gatherers

In their passion for completion, the devoted – dry-lidded,
holy and haunted – poke among the blasted pieces
for traces of what newspapers call "human remains"
but something, of course, will always be missing.

Impossible to get it all. All that once had a semblance
reassembled to be buried close to wholeness. As if they
can ever resemble themselves again. Leg by cell by
eyelash, they will be gleaned by the *hesed shel emet*

faithful who are hoisted aloft to lift human flesh
off the trembling leaves. Before the last light, the first star,
they will sift the shards of colossal explosives,
combing through tangles of rubber, singed wire,

glass, shoes, the body shells, every crumb of skin,
ash of hair, finger nail, the clotted blood, the cracked skull,
the broken armature of bones; they will climb the sides
of buildings carrying plastic bags filled with cotton balls

to blot the stunned bricks, the smoking windows.
While dazed mourners try to find a *minyan*, they will pick
at the bark of trees, scour flag poles, every house and
lamp post they pass to bundle up what once were children –

there are always children – busy women who shopped early
for produce still livid with soil, readers and smokers and men
who sold diamonds. Even if these burial crews come home
to their wives washed clean,

who wants a job like this, without pay, restless, sleepless,
their fingernails cut to the quick, their pockets emptied.
It is not written *You shall bury him intact,*
only *You shall bury him on the day he dies.* To do it right,

they would have to save the very air around the deed,
even the man who strapped explosives to his chest.
His severed head. His squandered heart.
Everything that belongs to each dead. The last blood

that leaves the body contains the soul, it is written.
The last breath contains the awe, the last sight an after-
image that cannot be imagined. Once bound to the task,
they must gather with charity all that is commingled: the killer

and the killed, when one left home to board the bus,
the bomb hidden, the infant held, the terrible misconception
of the teaching, the non-believer settled in beside the devout,
the words they were about to utter to each other, the sweet

subtext of country. This is not a country easily divided
from the body. Because every Jew carries it, it scatters;
Jews have been found in cellars, their scrolls in caves,
their rituals in Mexico. An exploded bus is a Torah destroyed.

The gatherers, meticulous to the point of madness, are like
crows in the field. Avid and silent at their work, they bring back
to their young their stories which are passed *l'dor vador*,
from mouth to mouth to mouth...........

Angles

A Palestinian Arab is shooting my daughter.
Circling her for advantage, he works his way around obstacles,
keeps her locked in the cross-hairs of his sight.
Now he is able to see her head-on and in the round,
he can pick his moment.
Indulging his trained maneuvers, she smiles and smiles
for him.
It is her wedding day. He has assured us
he has photographed Jewish weddings many times,
he understands our rituals, when to film, when to look away.
I watch my daughter in his hands.
He twists the lens, zooms her closer, he's got her
mugging, relaxed, nothing but marriage on her mind.

SACRED GRAFFITI

Agapanthus, Jacaranda, Bougainvillea

I wasn't born in the San Fernando Valley, my beloved high school
in the South Bronx is closing forever, forever, I could dance
to that stunted riff, I could cry. Where are the girls who sang
Gilbert and Sullivan, where are the tenors? I met one once, he
served me pizza in Queens. I hoped he was on his way. I was
on the way to transit, crossed the country in a '53 Olds. surprised
how bleak Texas was, how red was Missouri – or was it Kansas?
Missouri was so quiet, we had to leave a restaurant when my
baby screamed bloody murder. We got to L.A. in May, the month
agapanthus blooms. I didn't notice, I was still crying. I missed
my mother. I missed the subway and the New York Public Library
where I was once seduced by a sharpie who said he liked the hair
on my arms. I couldn't name the trees. We bought a house with
an orange tree. We thrilled ourselves. We went back to New York
on a brisk day in March. We couldn't go back. We were welcomed
but everyone had closed themselves over the gap we left, we were
bulky, we were cold and inconvenient, we slept in guest rooms
and ate in Korean restaurants, we were no longer cosmopolitan, we
owned plants no one had heard of, they couldn't even picture
agapanthus, the plethora of purple debris left on the ground by
lavish jacarandas, the cerise profusion of bougainvillea. To them
profusion is clotted living, thick-packed citizens on Fifth Avenue
in the afternoon, I'm not being pejorative, I enjoy pushing to get
somewhere, I like the sensible grid of Manhattan, I'll always find
the Museum of Modern Art, it is pitched where it was, winning
its war with Jackson Pollock's randomness as proof of an eclectic
coexistence though I think they moved the Rousseau.
You know which one.

        It was still March when I got back to L.A.,
the whole valley suffused with the scent of citrus, my mind reeling,
my feet dancing as if I had chosen the right partner, ivy at last
supporting a north wall once held up only by graffiti signatures.
How brave and inquiring are the purple umbels of agapanthus,

someone brought them here from Africa, someone snipped a sprig of bougainvillea from some wet loam in South America, smuggled it in in a raincoat pocket; anyone who's ever tripped over a broken eucalyptus branch knows that God walked across oceans to get here. Spanish names on the boulevards. If I remember the waltz and the two-step, I can be at home anywhere. I saw similar shrubs in Italy. I drank that same red wine in Hungary.

Thinking About

that day last week when I was walking along
and found thirty-six cents lying in the street. Not
in one spot, as if a kid had inadvertently dislodged parts
of his lunch money – one quarter, one dime, one cent –
but opulently, cash crashing from the sky like Godtalk.
I found the quarter first, in a place generally sparking
shards of broken glass and leaves sparkling
with sprinkler water; it's a wonder I saw it at all.
The dime lay sideways in a crack not far away
but definitely not proximate, and later,
almost as an afterthought, the still shiny penny.
I tease my sister who travels mornings on a treadmill
instead of striding like I do through daily weather changes –
could you find 36 cents on your living room carpet?
It was days later I ran into an old acquaintance
who gave me some news that maybe will change my life,
the place where we met as unlikely a rendezvous
as the confluence of coins on a long path,
the words on my mind more unlikely than the usual
songs I hum that seem to come from nowhere.
When she called out my name, I'd been praying
for directions, and I mean it not in the rote drone
of conventional prayer but in the anguish of drought,
and she brought me a sentence. After hours of mulling
it over, light curved back around the bend saying *thirty-
six cents, dope*, thirty-six is twice eighteen, the number
consistent with Life in the Kabbalistic numerology of
LIFE in the Torah, and LIFE DOUBLED certainly gets
your attention. What are the odds of 36 cents raining on you
like confetti? And didn't that accidental woman
have to call out my name twice? In the days that followed,
I began to notice more. I found information everywhere.

Step into the Mojave at Noon

simplicity, and beauty, and inevitable grace…
                      William Wordsworth

The desert dissembles, resembles the skeleton
      of a planet: its desiccated bones,
           its gravel, its ground scored
                like tombstones by dying rivers.
                    A heat that rises palpable as water.

And yet, things move, cactus blooms.
      Here is the wind arousing our hair, livening
           our skulls, troubling the sparse grasses; a locust
                poses long enough to flash
                    indigo, smoke, amber.

We have stepped in human, parched for omens
      while chaos chords
           as song, a dry gust
                hisses past our cheek,
                    dust in our shoes, mercy
                        under our feet.

It is possible to grow ancient in minutes, or die
      into a flower. Thirst
           moves from the throat to the heart
              and is slaked through the eyes
                  where mirages and miracles overlap.

We adapt like stones in gardens that shelter rebel crops,
      yielding will to merge
           with the sun
              and our breath is the sign of merging
                  and the burn is the singe of healing.

Humming

I tend to hum in supermarkets. My daughter hears me two
aisles away. She asks whether I know the market's song.
She's being sarcastic. I thought by now she'd outgrown her
unwillingness to be seen with me. She makes me question
what I'm doing. Am I praising or praying earth's syncopation
back to itself, scoping its music until the hum becomes a hymn
sung in layers like the *ohms* in the throats of Tibetan monks.

The other day I listened to a mass for four voices in a Gothic
church. Because they sang a cappella, I became the organ and
the chimes, I was the wooden pews worn to satin, I the
melancholy saints, I, the flames, the shadows, I, the coins.
I was the supplication. Last night I heard a rabbi sing a word
so softly it was sister to a hum, and the word was *ruach*,
the word for spirit and the word for wind.

Thanks to you who have brought my humming to my attention,
who get that sometimes my hum is a whistle in the dark and
sometimes it's grieving. You have helped me know how one
sound sets another in motion, how thunder and gun shots are
different tolling, why this earth is always shaking, though I must
be honest, you haven't quite shown me the source of that final
quake, the one for which I seem to be rehearsing.

Revisiting Ozymandias

    A sculpture, *The Last Supper* by A. Szukalski,
        imbedded in the shifting isolation of the Nevada desert

Each figure faces a different direction
like leaves keyed to the gifts of God's light; it is
the illusion of center that will move even sunflowers
against force fields of personal desire.
What does it mean to be astonished
by El Greco's knowledge of agony, ten hours
of sitar music drawing the mind toward madness
or that goofy smile on the faces of saints?
If I met perfection in the desert,
I'd expect it to be a wistful Ozymandias
on the way to total distintegration,
but I'd recognize it, and its imprint, and its echo, and its argument.

At the last supper, someone must have told a joke,
just to break the tension, and someone else
insisted on correctness. Each job was chosen,
each assigned, each essential. Knowing this,
I don't empty my heart in despair. For this picture
has been repeated over and over, thirteen ghosts,
pallid shrouds, what the artist must give over to entropy
and what the poet grabs and hides inside
her mouth. Be grateful it is white as a new mind,
moored to the desert floor. If it is obscured
by dust storms or an impatient foot on the gas,
you can always rely on the photograph
left on the inner eye of the bug in the rock
that you carry, on the shadow
left by candlelight on the half-moon of your nail.

Landscape with Wounded Bird

In this other life I live,
I pick up the bird and bring it home.
It nestles near my heart as if it could
assume the beat.
I mix mud, seeds, and roots into balm
and repair its crushed wing
in the manner of twelve-year-olds
gifted with grace.
After it is whole, I let it go
and watch it soar.
As it rises it bursts into flame,
disappears so fast,
heaven must be in its sight,
but it swoops right back and lands
on my still-open palm,
ruby-plumed, sapphires in its beak.

In the life which I live,
with smaller risks and smaller joys,
I don't touch the bird.

Hitchhiker

I waved my hand as if she were a floater
inside my eye. I brushed her
away, one of those lost unkempt souls
you see stranded at bus benches trailing
their parcels of loose ends.
Impatient or sick or bereft, not wanting
or able to wait, she showed me
by gesture and nods and pushing
her body toward my car door it wouldn't be far,
she meant no harm, she didn't belong
to a gang, she needed a ride
and nothing more. By the next light,
where I was forced to stop,
I knew I had been wrong to raise an arm
so swiftly. I knew I'd stopped thinking
as soon as I saw her and kept driving,
shaking my head, justifying, lying
to myself that she could have robbed
me, you never know.
No sooner had I fled the scene,
I began to play the game of what if.
I began to take credit
for that spontaneous kindness.
I began to feel that high I might have gotten
from that low I'd sunk down into
in the leather seat of my brand new Volvo.
I began to play with a memory already receding.
I can no longer tell you what she was wearing.
In the murky realm of false witnesses,
the story keeps changing.
Don't even ask me what street I was on.

From a Penitent's Hand

There is a plant called crown of thorns,
leafless, spiky, clotted with red
                                  flowers.

Once it grew outside my house. Now
it lives inside my head, scratching, scratching
                                  to get out.

Wings

A Monarch butterfly is trapped under the eaves.
Its tribe is dying off.
I reach across species, tell it to be still,
get it to sit a millisecond on the soft fuzz of a feather duster
so I can lift it to safety,
but it goes right back to its struggle like a punch-drunk boxer.
Every time I come close, it revs its wings with a speed that turns it black.
Finally it stalls, like a small plane
that seems to lose its heart to the sky's implacable size.
The next morning, there it is, so quiet
I'm afraid it has wedded itself to the wood and died a mosaic.
But it is alive,
and I don't know how to set myself free.

You Remind Me of Someone

Du Oder Ich (You or Me) a painting by Maria Lassnig

Your skin's the canvas of your lacerations.
Sometimes your body deflates,
as if death stole the viscera before you died.
Sometimes it grieves.
Always it betrays – twisting, aging.
An internal necrosis shades your singular contour,
decomposing in a harrowing you limn with color.
You skin yourself alive.
Pain is sometimes yellow, like the halo surrounding
a healing bruise.
Sometimes it is a fish-like aquamarine.
Your orange thighs, the breasts, the vagina.
You could have said you dwell in beauty,
this is your true face, the mask
you wear to the Monster Ball.
No lie can hide you at ninety,
no adjective save you.
A tourist in Vienna, I stumble on your paintings
hung the height of a woman's body
and room enough to bring me to my knees.
You command me to read you.
That much sudden agony.
Then I am home,
wrestling a language that begs to render
a futile compassion.
My body of work fails me.
Ill-equipped to translate itself
in black letters on space,
it makes black merely black.
Do you think anyone sees my tongue?
 – e.g., your painting titled *You or Me…*

where each hand points a gun....
It would take a novel, a trilogy,
a fucking Britannica!
Surely my body is something like yours.
My flesh dissolves at the very same edges.
I should be afraid.
I should rise from my chair
and roll on the ground. I should scream.

Marrowbones

The fat women in the Coney Island steam bath
        pinched my cheek and laughed at nothing,
sweat gleaming off their skin and coarse, curly hair,
        not a bone to be seen anywhere,

not in my aunt's long breasts, none in the flesh
        of my mother's belly. I grew up in the shelter
of kitchen gossip, amplitude nourished by yeasty smells,
        pillows of soft rising dough, a feminine language

that taught me where the body begins, its armature
        concealed, its health augmented like good soup.
By sixth grade, I knew I was fat. I married a man
        with a flat stomach and an unrequited hunger.

The soup the Nazis fed him in their concentration camp
        was thin as silk, what floated there thinner still.
From the aunts and mothers I learned wisdom is fluid,
        rescue, a recipe they give to their daughters.

When the soup is done, I remove the bones,
        scoop out the glutinous marrow, every last shred.
I spread it on fresh rye bread.
        I watch him eat, and my heart gets fat.

Anguish

There's a man waiting for me to lay down
my pen, and it is not you.
His presence in my bed says
we won't be discarded now
that our friends and lovers are dead,
even if we are strangers to one another.
After you died and I was left breathing,
the charge that glows off skin
in the dark drove me so far past you,
I could no longer keep what was us.
I rub the man's back, plunge my fingers
into his hair, knead his shoulders.
My hands shake with their lack of knowledge.
I practice like a swimmer in shark-filled waters,
loving here, where blood has been spilled.

The reason I don't visit your grave

is hidden – the grave marked by a bronze plaque
sunken under the brink of sod, sort of invisible,
even when I'm coming close, stumbling
over others, stepping on who knows whose
remains. Even when I've fallen to my knees,
when I've found it, and I'm winded and sobbing,
I know this is not the reason I don't grieve
the way some do, randomly or weekly, or on certain
anniversaries bring flowers or stones
or tokens whose myths are known only to us.
The smoky highway view?
– I put you there, then sold the house,
moved away, taking only two drawers,
which you permeate. Maybe I'm afraid
when I arrive out of breath, I will have to admit
there's a hole in my day, that tick of the clock
when I used to shift from solitude to expectation,
when I began to gather the vegetables,
slice them into small circles, season
to suit your taste, our tastes for years
having yearned toward each other's
until they met and we wanted the same;
so I stirred the pot, kept one eye on the flame,
one eye on the hour, my ear cocked
for your sound. No, it isn't that
sorrow, which follows me in and out
of my sleep, and I have no fear of ghosts –
God, I'd love to make a date
to drink wine with your ghost. I thought,
if I could eradicate all reason,
maybe I could recover my bigger heart,
a longer view
linked to centuries of habitual grave-diggers,

Hebrews who buried their dead
in caves, Egyptians who wrapped them first
as if heaven awaited the surprise of these gifts.
Maybe it's the proximity of my parents
that stops me from coming by, or the two
bare spaces my sister keeps, one for herself,
one for her dead marriage.
Once we were a package deal,
six gravesites side by side, and now,
it's more family than I want crowding me.
Maybe I'll figure it out when I lie down
in the empty place next to you,
wait and see who visits,
who brushes away the stray grass
like errant wisps of hair.
Are you still listening? I tend to digress.
It's your grave I started with, but no one escapes
the family business. Joseph thought he was safe
in Egypt, never dreamed of reconciliation, yet
when his burly brothers bowed before him,
familiar strangers with their imperfect motives
tangled in their hearts like unsorted wool,
Joseph wept.
      You came to us empty-handed,
your parents' grave a chimney in Auschwitz,
your siblings, dust somewhere. You came
with your nightmares of resurrection
and we took you in;
in being and in absence, you remain with us,
you will always be with us,
so when I visit your grave, we are not alone,
we are in the burial cave with our family bones,
we are in the turmoil of cross-purposes;
but home by myself on this cold winter night,
we visit in privacy, and quietly, catch up.

Deep Inside the Silence I Hate, the Silence I Love

I go through my rooms in the dark without stumbling,
familiar as a cat with the coffee table,
calmed by its solid dimensions,
the text of hushed contrasts, cold wood under my bare feet,
the prickle from rugs I spread to muffle the floor.

Yet it is sweet to hear sound in a house where one lives alone,
the walls settling into the vault of earth,
a puzzled fly's sizzle at the window.
Something euphoric is trying to enter through a cleft.
I won't deny it, I'm afraid.

Sometimes wind shoulders past the door.
The softest footfall gets louder than blood in the ear.
What would I give up for the friction
of human language, the flesh and argument of company?

A woman praised my roses, their musk and tinge and placement
in a crystal vase. Though she had not struck its brittle edge,
her words went clamoring
through every room. When she left,
the air closed around her space, and I moved freely through.

Smoking With My Father

In those days I could have poise
for the cost of a cigarette, so
I enlisted the help of my father.
Eager to reopen the door shut
when I entered adolescence,
he taught me the skills of smoking.
He'd clear his throat with those
familiar little coughs, he'd take his time,
demonstrating deep inhalation,
masterful fingering. Years later
a man in a Max Beckmann painting
holding a cigarette European style
reminded me how my father and I
bonded, when I was sixteen,
how I later dated and married
a smoking man, all of us too young
to take on the heat and grief of love
with our empty hands.

Honeydew in Season

As soon as I'm pierced by the shock of its sweetness,
its unearthly dissolve, the soft bleed at the end of the spoon,
I'm swept into sorrow. That's how split-second quick it was.
Absent joy before it can be swallowed. Here is the summer of 1947,
corn and watermelon, sweat on the roof of sleepless nights,
a neighbor's shouts announcing adult strife, the heat's craze,
long days with nothing to do, long free books from the library,
long walks and late dusk talks with my sister, everything
endless except the melting ice cream, the long line of ants.
How can I hold a ghost of what is falling away, passing
from a full mouth into a swoon of ripe happiness.
We made it last three days, we cut each slice smaller.
I thought it would take years before summer stayed hardly at all.

Boxing the Beast

The desire to own
the sleek stunning symmetry of it, to keep it, boxed up,

for yourself alone: you can't resist
even the illusion

though you know the perfect tiger ten feet away
is a million miles beyond your art.

So you keep shooting, frame after frantic frame,
while stalking nothing but a reflection,

its yellow eyes unforgiving,
the silent grace that quivers

just above the screaming grass.

GHOST TATTOO

My Mother's House

My mother's house is gone from here
        where I stand not the exact spot which I don't know
was never told I never asked

but somehow have the village name
        which is hard to say after some syllables
got sheared across borders past Hungary's eastern edge

became Ukraine the language so scraped the burghers broke pens
        to spell it broke teeth to say it
chained their leaders changed their dances

though paprikash and cabbages still reigned
        I'm sure it was near these falling-down hovels she said
wedged low in front of a green tall mountain

beside a small river, really a stream so cold
        it kept meat fresh from winter to summer.
I can hardly breathe. Why this joy when she is long dead?

Is it because I know something I never knew before
        and still don't?
But I am here, and whatever of her she left before she left,

that child, those sisters,
        the brother that went off to war and came home
addled, the orphan she became, that barefoot life,

what it is to live in snow and planting seasons,
        what it is to dig into the earth, milk a cow,
fear soldiers on horses,

drunken neighbors with mouths full of curses,
        that's still here, I feel it, her fear,
I feel her here.

We've Taken Care of Everything

My sister and I have picked out our coffins, I told my son-in-law
Paul, we've pre-paid the cost of digging the graves, the grave liners,
the washing of the bodies, the ushers, the guest book, you know
what's involved, so we don't put that burden on our kids the way we
had to take on our parents' last choices three months apart,
first our mother, that was over forty years ago, we went together,
even laughing at times in that giddy way of sisters, in that self-
conscious way when someone else's grief is still hanging in the chill
air of the coffin room, no more than hours had passed, we looked
around, the soft lighting, the levitated caskets, cheaper ones at the
bottom, and at the top, the brass fittings and good mahogany, some
lids open to show white satin pillows, and we couldn't help it, we
started laughing, I mean we were hysterical, cracking jokes, kind of
working off each other, so we decided we wouldn't let our children
go through that, we went together,
more sober this time, we picked out the same pine boxes,
bland as the wooden boxes cream cheese came in when we were
kids, leaving little to hinder the body's passage back into the earth.
When I told Paul my sister and I have taken care of everything,
he asked me, what about your daughters,
don't you think they should be given those hours,
making arrangements, the hours you and your sister spent together?

Caesarean Birth, Mid-Twentieth Century

The cut to Aurelia, mother of Caesar, was only a myth,
    but, my impeccable first daughter, I was
sliced open, and you were ripped out pink and bawling,
    to save us both.

Someone showed me toenails, too swift to take in,
    then whisked you away,
would not let me claim you nine heartsick days. Some rumor
    of contagion afflicting the corridors.

    They taught me sneaking.
I soft-slippered down to the nursery window; I think I waved
    but the doctors held sway,
slipped pills into my food, the way they do with prisoners.

    They dried my milk.
How do I swathe you in lost time? Every night you call
    around eleven. For uncounted minutes,
we talk about our fevers.

My two daughters drop me off at the museum

go for a walk if they were here I'd show them this painting
begun with a photograph a woman at her loom a woman
probably Chinese the artist's name old-fashioned wooden
loom could be bamboo the cloth she has woven falling
folding the painting teeming with allegorical birds do you think
what are you two talking about it's windy are they dressed
warm enough they are fine I am alone with their absence not all
of my eccentricities known to them when my mother died I thought
my father would burst into bloom but he died three months later
she is stoic intact her heart tucked inside beyond her lips
as drips and washes dissolve the photo the painting splits
she is a pillar she is still rooted her trees scatter their birds
leaflike the walls sprout flowers look. Look. Cross the street
carefully I love San Francisco you idiot they are grown women
they are married they have children their children grown I love
the way the painting derives a life from her interiority
am I the only one enthralled here while memory is passing
into history and the birds flock across the canvas escaping
their plumage pulsing a wing a feather a claw but you do get it
the mystery of her inner myth complete I better keep track
they gave me 90 minutes we will meet in the lobby I should be
done by then that is what they did in New York
would not come inside the Whitney to look at the Rothkos
I never taught them how to look at a Rothko how could I
when scant time's left to browse from here there's only drift
what is there about this woman is it the concentration I think
it must be the incongruity maybe that's too blatant you know
about the creative process or day-dreaming or how she is going to
pay the rent no one standing next to me I am so lucky having
good weather and this is what I wanted to be celebrated on my
eightieth birthday with my two daughters no husbands no children
and I got to see this astonishing painting

Zachary's Rainbow

Who named it teal,
          Cayuga duck dazzle-dressed to fit the marsh it's sitting in?
My ocean's sometimes denim,
                often mauve, the shade inside a wave's turn.

Who said rouge,
          blush on a cheek, labial pink of the Angelique tulip?
Why is a rainbow called hope?

My grandson's color blind.
            His world is gray, lights and darks only, no cerise or
            butterscotch,
all his ice cream ashen, his gold retriever silver.

I want to ask him
        do you harbor wild parrots in your sleep?
And the auroras I see dancing in your eyes—aren't they the dawning
                          of imagination?

Mystics and Mathematicians Crowd the Shore

The complexion of waves,
a whale hides in plain sight then shows itself: a single spray
sun-rinsed, thicker than rain.

Too often I've looked away too soon,
but this time I pick a spot and stick to it until, like Moses
seeking the face of God, I am given a glimpse of the whale's back.

Denied revelation of all the rest, flukes and function, its actual size,
I know what Moses guessed: the price of his disbelief.
I sense what Jacob could not comprehend before he went to sleep,

his head laid on rocks, his feet curled in prayer. At dawn he rose
and named the site God's house. Maybe something gritty in the dust,
not unlike the fossil of a dream,

told him how a trace stands for the whole.
I won't complain.
I take my place with those who saw the gleam

and had to fathom its domain. I point and laugh, I do that little dance.
Then I thank the sea for opening herself
which lets me keep on working, ink on paper, imagining the deep.

Stephen Hawking's Reasoning

Hawking's body is a stem stuck in earth,
and he figures out how something came from nothing.

Inert as a tree trunk in a universe spewing
like a drunkard beyond its own boundaries

he reports back through his computer *there is no god*.
Havoc has no reason.

Surely Hawking's random genius grasps an irony
in which he praises nothing and is praised,

blames and thanks no one for a brain
that speeds as fast as light, and glows.

The Critical Angle of Sunlight

Bosch emblazoned his savage imagination
with anal bouquets and bird-headed beasts;
and cruel-stemmed trees are named Angelica.

The dart-poison frogs of Central America,
the blacks green-banded, the lapis-blues, the ochers
sparking like lustrous gems, kill on touch.

They darken the sky. In the rupture between
ice poles and craters, motorists crash, wreckage
a rainbow of shadows, and camphor-weed glows.

The sun blares out at last. The color of blood
is always red. Ah, today's winds have shattered
my thoughts; epiphany's on my mind.

My mild old friend confesses he owns a gun.
A woman I like is dying, she's doped on morphine,
and I won't see her blue-green eyes again.

Picasso's Four Bulls

He begins with a bull, a bull
you and I would see as ordinary,
solitary, stood sideways, feeding like
a still life or pawing the worn-out ground
in a bullring, weighing its stake.

The ink will stick to the drawing to make
a lithograph of a bull, fully depicted, horns,
hulk shaped and shadowed, swinging sex and
tail, you will feel them bristling, and notice
its one dumb eye, its minacious head.

This bull won't be enough for Picasso.
He'll angle off, I doubt he stood back
more than a minute before he cubed
the second bull with a butcher's hand,
bulked it up, kept its menace.

Kept its hazard as it got more abstract,
his genius paradox, allusion; also valor, the
horns more erect, the tail thicker, swishier;
hide, hooves and scrotum augmented.
Even the ears. More face, two eyes.

Then he flays it. Takes away one eye.
Straightens the haunch, streamlines the legs.
With the hooves gone and the tail fallen,
muscles shorn, there's more light, less shadow,
and still, a bull, until he gets to the final bull.

Just lines, lines, lines, no shading, no fillers,
the eye a small miracle of understatement,
the two horns made one in a single swoop,
elliptical, almost comical, the tail and sex
simple hints. Now, now you can tell his truth.

Masks

I never liked Halloween,
when I had to choose
a single disguise; so many lies
left out.

Shoe Confessions

If only Neruda had glorified pumps instead of cucumbers.
If Keats had immortalized one pair of wedgies.
I would not need to dredge memory for metaphor.
My baby shoes, never bronzed, are history.

I turned thirteen.
My mother bought me the shoes I loved best.
Some dark green nappy fabric, cinnamon leather trim.
She gave me grassland and ground.

I grew tall and taller, bobbled on stiletto heels.
Some saw my eyes, some looked below my knees.
A man fell in love with my notorious instep.
A man stroked my boots while we watched *Tosca*.

I danced in red shoes, left them on a doorstep in Calcutta.
Aroused a foot fetishist passing by.
My husband, a voyager, wanted to be American.
Ate fried Spam. Left me his collection of blue suede shoes.

Lunatics Love Neruda

Twenty years apart, two lunatics gave me copies of Pablo Neruda's *Twenty Love Poems and a Song of Despair.* Inscribed them with tidings straight out of their soiled hearts. One swore not to hurt me, and branded me with scars of betrayal, which I sometimes pass along. The other scribbled Greek or Hebrew letters across the first four pages, who could tell what from what, their scattered angles obscuring their truth. He'd walked out of Barnes and Noble without paying for the book, a small crime in context. Shouldn't I be grateful each year swallows the years that have gone before? Time passes otherwise undigested, in break-out flash-backs. One day, filing like a librarian instead of a fatalist, I come across the two books, as if one had given birth to the other, their twinned presence reminding me I'd never read Neruda's love poems! What a morning, to be granted a second chance, to read the master in maturity. To be given the gift of pause. To pardon the reckless promises humans make in unguarded handwriting. Age makes desire manageable. It is possible to visit Neruda for the first time, possible to fall into his mercy, the way I dropped from the womb into somebody's outstretched arms.

Nameless Flowers, Anonymous Trees

When I moved here, I saw the tarnished silvers, greens
torn down to brown by wind and wear, but I couldn't name them
until I had peered into the faces of my neighbors, and then
mystery broke into agapanthus, impatiens, manzanita, invasive
yellow mustard, sage, chaparral, and golden yarrow, and

in the gullies, pale wistfulful clusters of narrow-leaved milkweed,
food and harbor for the Monarch butterfly, its fuzzy foliage
nature's whisperer, which, at the height of their bliss, tells them
it's time to mount the wind, and move on.

Where I grew up, trees were anonymous, they seemed accidental,
a random seed, a crack in the sidewalk, rain, but we kids knew
Wedgewood blue lilacs outside the flower shops, fragrant intoxicant
on Mother's Day. My fourth grade teacher favored ferns cascading
over the window sills like chips of clay glazed with celadon.

One early spring morning, right outside my classroom window
an unnamed tree flaunted a liquid green so thin the sun piercing
an infant leaf passed right through it, landing on my right hand.
I sat there until it told me *it's time to go.*

Announcement

I should compose my own ending before I'm embalmed
in bromides, misconstrued in inelegant prose. I should

dope out the *comme il faut* approach: humble or sumptuous,
a Neruda hallelujah or a tenebrous Buddha.

Whether I'm frayed like a blazer in Dorian Gray's closet
or spent like the work boots in a Van Gogh still life

the tenderfoot doctors will bray what their youth doesn't get:
you're doing fine.

What the good doctors mean is
I don't have the afflictions that killed Keats

and Rimbaud, poets whose dying burned through
their epochs with green wine and shortened sentences

while I am given extra decades and retirement goals,
and many more pills than my parents had.

Back in the seventies, we smoked, confessed,
spoke in glossolalia, wrote our own obituaries.

It was fun at forty-one or two flinging our lives
forty years into the future:

how many books we'd mothered, the good we'd done.
Now the veracious denouement comes knocking.

A grandchild reads Tarot cards, but won't do mine.
They know my life's not found in the flip,

not in the Death or the Priestess cards, but somewhere
in the cloud, written out in longhand, and still unlived.

About the Author

Florence Weinberger was born in New York City, raised in the Bronx, educated at Hunter College, California State University, Northridge and UCLA, and has worked as a teacher, legal investigator and consumer advocate. She is the author of five published collections of poetry, *The Invisible Telling Its Shape*, *Breathing Like a Jew*, *Sacred Grafitti* and *Ghost Tattoo*. Five times nominated for a Pushcart Prize, and for Best of the Net, her poetry has appeared in a number of literary magazines, including *The Comstock Review*, *Antietam Review*, *Rockvale Review*, *Nimrod*, *Poetry East*, *Solo*, *Rattle*, *Baltimore Review*, *The Los Angeles Review*, *Cultural Weekly*, *Calyx*, *Miramar*, *The River Styx*, *December*, *Another Chicago Magazine*, *North American Review*, *The Los Angeles Review*, *Salt*, *Epoc hand Shenandoah*.

Her poems have also been published in many anthologies, including *Blood to Remember: American Poets on the Holocaust*, *Truth and Lies That Press For Life*, *Invocation LA*, *The New Los Angeles Poets*, *Ghosts of the Holocaust*, *Grand Passion: Images from the Holocaust*, *Claiming the Spirit Within*, *Lifecycles V. 2*, *The Cancer Poetry Project*, *Pandemic Puzzle Poems*, *So Luminous the Wildflowers*, and *The Widows' Handbook*. Among awards are first prizes in the *Poetry/LA Bicentennial*, *Sculpture Gardens Review*, *Mississippi Valley*, *Red Dancefloor* and the dA Center for the Arts poetry contests. She served as a judge for the PEN Center USA Literary Contest.

www.ingramcontent.com/pod-product-compliance
Lightning Source LLC
Chambersburg PA
CBHW031155160426
43193CB00008B/382